POEMS FORMAL
AND INFORMAL

from a long lifetime

Clare Campbell

Published in 2000 by Cassandra Press

20 Little Meadow
Bar Hill,
Cambs.CB3 8TD

ISBN 0 9508829 8 4

by the same author

Only Begotten Sonnets   ISBN 0 7135 0213 4
Shakespeare's Sonnets edited as a continuous sequence
ISBN 0 7135 1897 X
ISBN 0 8476 6134 2
Bell & Hyman (U.K), Rowman & Littlefield (U.S.A.) 1978

Text volume reissued by Cassandra Press 1999
ISBN 0 9508829 5 X

Conquest of Angels (novel about a music festival)
ISBN 0 9508829 6 8
The Century of Optogen (a history of the future)
ISBN 0 9508829 7 6
ed. and contrib.
To Sing Out Sometimes, Poems of a Family
ISBN 0 9508829 0 9
The Unkindest Beast, An Anthology for Animal Aid
ISBN 0 9508990 0 3

Drawing on end page by Adrian Campbell

Text processing by N. McLeod and Nichola Beeson

Printed by RPM Technical Print
5 Haviland Road, Wimborne, Dorset BH21 7RZ

Foreword

I prefer formal poems on the whole, having sung in choirs all my
life so that I hear words with very exact rhythms and pitches.
Dons who discount the musical side of poetry get it wrong; Latin
and Greek poetry was defined by crotchets and quavers. I have
aimed to put informal poems mainly on left-hand pages, but
fewer of them seemed worth a place, and sometimes translations
or things written for fun stand there instead. In my later poems
the two styles tend to converge.

The subject-matter is roughly in chronological order, though the
dates of writing in each group vary widely. The main groups are:
- war and peace (the war broke out when I was 19); retrospect on
falling in love (this contains the earliest poems which are all
formal - neither my reading nor my poet parents were modernist,
and I loved lucidity as I still do); music and musicians; private
loneliness and global horrors; family love; old age as unfinished
business. My political poems are not misandrist: anyone would
hate machismo who had a father as gentle as mine. My love
poems are not lesbian: the raison d'etre of hetero love is
procreation, homophil love having different springs may not
want to imitate that. I kept in touch with the addressee of these
poems; she particularly liked the poem which stands last in this
book. The image of a mystical journey recurs throughout. The
poems make best sense read in their printed order.

I have translated Lieder for recitals and broadcasts by the
distinguished tenor Ian Partridge. In song vowels generally last
much longer than consonants, so that to rhyme the vowels only is
valid for the ear (Dylan Thomas does this in Fern Hill; students
don't notice that it rhymes at all). Song also brings out how much
alliteration helps audibility. I sometimes stress prepositions,
which prissy people dislike though it is natural to vernacular
English, e.g. "the washing úp"; "weed wide enough to wrap a
fairy in". I enjoy syncopating spondees and phrasing by caesura
(word-end). One writes poetry from a love of technology, surely,
as well as a dire need to say the unsayable.

Cassandra

Ancient Greek women
Were allowed to be interested in the truth
Provided they threw a fit of hysterics
And said a god told it tó them.
Oh let me even on this last page of history
Have the salvation of a seizure,
Let me appear on television foaming
With the after-signs of an orgasm so interesting
Even the football fans will watch,
While not of course shifting in their armchairs,
And say, the god must know.
This is not female do-gooding, it is Cassandra, it is
      extra-sensory perception,
Messages, which even a meek typist cannot but take down.
Take some dictation, Miss Cassandra: said the god
Or bird.
Troy is doomed. Go, go, go
Tonight. Pack no bags.
Out into the trustful dark
Dissemble, hide ...

(Message disrupted)

They lied saying she was raped.
Pour décourager nous autres.
I have had one dreamn recurring a life long:
Virgin soldier broke from the cell
By a side-route no Freuds watch at,
Still on the run
Has not yet made it home to that grass-shored sea coast
The earthly paradise found lost,
But to date she is not recaptured.

Greater London

When the great town's redeemed into green meadow,
And moonflowers flutter where the tramlines clanged,
And the sky-outflanking chimneys have been laid low
Whose smoke now plumes the blue or the star-pronged
Dark: and that time shall surely sometime come:
Then shall be understood these present shadows
That make the fifth wall of our life's bare room.

Slaves of great Babylon, who build her towers,
Pull weakly on the rope; forgive each other
Sudden absentings during business hours,
Half-heartedness, unlove. The great Earth-mother
Has tendrils through your pavements, and thereunder
The selves time would not let you be lie buried
Biding, until her meekness shall inherit.

On a soft night I left the city

My footpad walk in crotchet time
Rebounded off the shut-eyed square
And all the souls of doors were closed to me

I had left a note for the milkman
(Afraid the hauntings of a million bottles
Might stretch a dotted line by which to keep me taped)
"No more normality till Further Notice."

The football sun goes down
Shrugged in a jersey of cloud-fog
It is cold to have no home-going.

There was once a place, of course,
That I was shelved in, like the others,
Not the open disgrace of a tramp on the benches

But there comes a time
When no fire thaws and no roof heals the wind
That is the real night.

Oudeis at Sea

They dragged the sea and found only
Fishbones (unidentified) and a pair
Of rowing sculls; these should have floated
But must have rotted through
(Pearls at their eye-sockets) -
Boat they found no trace of,
Body still less.
But I did set out that day
Calm it was, shining, gloating almost,
Behind the veils a laugh in its throat,
Sea like an open hand waiting,
Uncurling its fingers (what have I got hidden
At my back?) now one hand now the other
In teasing wave-play
And I answered
I have always played in earnest,
And I did set out
Expecting fair-play weather
And the verdict still wide open.

The sea was very black and grey
The sea can storm for many a day.

The sea was marbled green and white
And talking to itself all night,

The fishes scintillant like stars
Dozed upon the deep sand-bars.

Of my long boat passed overhead
The fishes not a whisper said.

Xenos 1   **The Double Self**

Come enter in, I am all laid at ease
In this calm island of the living storm.
My curtains are hung round with reveries,
Come enter you within and make you warm,
I go not forth, but come and enter in,
I shall not fetch you home across the seas
But see my light, but in your darkening din
Tire of the voyage, and remember peace.
One stepped abroad, one went that should have stayed,
My Self, the inmate of my curtained sill;
I go not out to search, my patience frees
His spirit, but I keep his head-place laid:
Back they must carry him, if not until
The waters close over his obsequies.

Xenos means both host and guest.

Where shall I go to escape my cowardice?
Shall I cleave   the sky with mighty metal wings -
Start for the moor on winter evenings -
Becalm my boat in shoreless summer seas -

Where shall I go to escape my cowardice?
Shall I live alone, hungry with frozen limbs
(Where shall I go to escape my coward dreams)
And lock my spirit in eternal peace?

The more I dare the more my fear pursues.
Is it her strength that does my heart appal,
Her power over herself, her right to choose?
There's Everest to climb - "I am too small".
Why then resign, stay at the hearth and wait,
Be humbled unto heaven: "I am too great."

April 1939

Sonnet from the French

These were my times, a thousand years from you
I died: still hunted, still outside the net.
Human nobility was chained, and through
A masque of slaves I moved inviolate.
These were my times, yet I knew free repose,
I watched the flow of streams and soil and heaven
Circling me in precarious equipoise,
Had seasonable birds and honey given.

You who survive, how stands my heritage?
Have you contributed your harvest share?
Have you nostalgia for my fighting age?
Is my town richer because you live there?
Fear not I shall revisit you, survivor,
My flesh and spirit's hour's for ever over.

Translation of L'Epitaphe by Robert Desnos, 1900-1945. Desnos joined the French Resistance, and died "full of hope and projects" shortly after being liberated from Buchenwald.

Sister to Brother

When we were young, playing in the rocks and heather,
I timed my pace to yours,
Gave you a hand, my younger brother,
In the rough bits, eased aside the prickly gorse,
Seemed the harsh world's interpreter to you:
And now to save my world you're for the wars.

Then, skies and winds would challenge our endurance,
In tangled places we got lost at night;
New climbs or wider leaps opened their threat before us,
But all was safe and right
While my pulse raced in unison with you:
And now I'll sit in comfort while you fight.

Tent fires were starrier, woods denser,
Rivers more deep and strange, when we were there;
Unless we shared it nothing held adventure,
All held it, that we did but share:
And now you'll grapple the four winds to you
In some far country, I shall not know where.

Oh, it was not my way
To let you go ahead in tricky places,
Or fail a cheerful word to swing our flagging paces,
Or stay behind on a stiff day:
But all that's turned to purpose high in you
In me is just a child's remembered play.

Oh it's a crooked world, my brother;
I cannot follow where I ought to come:
Time's glass distorts me to a stay-at-home,
Life makes me give the lie to all we dared together,
Mocks my child's pride in trials, and on you
Has laid the toil of two.

So tramp ahead alone, my once companion;
And luck go by your side, instead of me;
And keep, oh keep the faith to see
Our true selves change not, constant beyond time's dominion,
Our goal stays single, and still close by you
My spirit troops, the whole long journey through.

The Marchers

We were lost on the small-cost expedition,
The million to one chance that must happen.
We did not witness acts of daring -
The alert was already over -
The veterans had sensibly taken cover -
Retreating death unpacked his load on us,
Turned back to pick us up as an afterthought.

The unnecessary, unexceptional dead.
There are generals planning great manoeuvres -
But we might have been you.
V.C.'s return from the deep-sea venture -
But your son coming home missed our ranks by chance,
And the thought will haunt him in the pub, at the dance:
Why should any be spared.
We are the logic at the heart of war -
Why should any be spared.

He that doeth it unto the least of these
Doeth it unto me.
In the street in the sky in the weeping fiancee at the window
I fall by a thousand ways of disaster.
The million to one chance is my certain sentence.
I am maimed of the leg that was his (there hesitant at the street
    crossing)
The stab of the Far East guerilla kicks me here in the spine.
See there,
I put those dead flowers in all those cemeteries;
Behold the white gardens of the living.
When one man dies there is no sense in the breath of the living:
How then shall one man die for the people?
But the people die in one man:
We were wounded for his transfusions,
We were wounded by his wounds.

You shut your ears from the tramp of our unknown feet
Because their sound is the truth.
You fumble for the special circumstance
That made us chosen for the pitiable,
You deafen your mind in the night a thousand miles from us
But our sound is the truth.
It is you it is you it is you that your wars have slain
And we come and we come and we come till war come not again.

The Robots

I was not silent when they tortured me.
I told them about truth and heaven and hell
And rage and panic and impossibility
Of conquest - oh, I told them all.

I showed them a blackbird sitting in the hedge,
Bronzed by the harmless fingers of the sun,
And children playing on a summer beach
I gave them, craving their compassion.

Slow soldering of the spirit's joints with lead
Sets in for many, as it had done for them.
I told them how their own eyes bled,
Their own hearts were singeing with my flame -

And then I saw they had no eyes, no hearts,
No senses, no inward parts.
Hollow robots of jangling tin
Cornered me in.

Then my tears broke in streams
Of deep relief.
I had dreamed that men are torturers, but dreams
Merit no belief.

Fire Raid

Out of the quiet of bedtime,
Time when a man would knock his pipe out
And we were dressing-gowned over the fire in my street,
Reading the book's last page
Before goodnight -
Came the rattle:
First the windowpanes, and in the air a faint shaking;
And we listened a little:
And then the blood-bursting clatter
Of the storm's breaking.
The din of violence shocked us at bedtime,
Anger came in a hurry,
Danger comes faster than expected
Ahead of the slow sirens
Out of the clouds in a snarling.
We wait for the others to receive it -
Death (but not us?) injury (but not us?)
We speculate:
And the crunching-thuds answer, a little distant.
There is a flickering-tongued fear from the gliding evil -
It whirrs away there into the dark north -
Brief doom is over.
Dark and wide again it heals over,
The silence that was too great for the brief-splitting anger -
And life is too great for us to remember killing.
A million waited, and those few came to an end -
The silence of them is lost in our numberless breathing.

But when we climbed upstairs from the shelter
To quiet again, leaned into the night air -
Staring each from our sill
We saw in a circle, red and silent,
From point to point puffing up in a mute ring round us,
Slow, blazing columns of disaster rolling,
Lighting our faces, with no noise.
And where they glowed,
(Pricking at our nostrils through the middle air),
There, cut to stabs of black, stood out far-seen
The steepled roof-lines, chimney and eave and tower
Still soaring in their crowd,
Alone with fire, standing proud.
And then the great clock struck,
Deep-echoing down the paths of night,

Unwavering in its vigil and its course,
His certain, usual voice
"My world of time goes on; be reassured."

So violent fires soon burn out themselves
Viewed from unmelted panes.

Service-man

("The mass of men lead lives of quiet desperation" Thoreau)

Don't pity me when shells are falling round,
Don't picture my set lips and call them brave,
Don't think I dream of love on this hard ground
Or dread the casual, unexpected grave.
Keep back your prayers, your pride, your tenderness,
This life's of steel, I could not need them less.

But when you see me strolling through the gate
To start the life that none calls hard to bear,
Dad's got a job for me, the girls a date,
And that's all over, things are what they were,
If then I flinch and cry aloud for aid,
Will there be pity for a man dismayed?

Oxford in Wartime

The cure of life, the cure of life, not here,
Not here between the orchards and the sky,
Where peace on earth and peace of mind appear
So easy, fields and minds in close ally;
Not with philosopher's attentive ear,
Not in authority's weighed wisdom, I
Have heard what should if anywhere be here,
Have solved the hieroglyphs of misery.
The master crafts, the master craftsmen, yes,
The keen and bloodless blade of scholarship,
Decorous achievement and benign address,
And reason's pleading against power's whip,
And sorrow's wonder hearing distant strife,
But here not here the cure, the cure of life.

Lament of the Employed

Don't let me fall in love with people seen in trains,
Or bother if it's fine, or listen when it rains,
Or follow out too far the presentiments of brains,
For I've got to get up when it's tomorrow.

Don't let me have scenes with insecure new friends,
Or get started on the sort of remarks that have no ends,
Or take a supper party to jazzy restaurants,
For I've got to get up when it's tomorrow.

Don't let me go to cinemas and dream that I'm a king
Of diamonds or stocks and shares or all that kind of thing,
And that I'm tall and handsome, and have a voice like Bing,
For I've got to get up when it's tomorrow.

I've been through enough hurricanes, pursued by men with
        knives,
And lived on desert islands with technicolour wives,
And picked out all the fruity bits of other people's lives
Who hadn't got to get up when it's tomorrow.

Don't let me make a plan; for a plan should be pursued,
And makes you push your fellows from the way, and be rude,
And robs you of the breakfast-time complaisance that is good
If you've got to get up when it's tomorrow.

Don't let me go to church - unless I go a lot,
But with lamplit singing in a strange town, not;
Or get lost in the woods when the year's going out,
For I've got to get up when it's tomorrow.

O turn my back to the light and put the angels out of sight,
And cast a dulling shadow on the words that poets write,
And leave off, strange callings to me heard in the night,
For I've got to get up when it's tomorrow.

Night Haul
(London postwar)

From every corner of the square
Glares a conspiracy of cats;
    The mouselike winds run warmly round;
    Through twinkling dust of traffic sound
    And radio from the lidless eyes of flats
    There drones the beat of summer air.

    Down the dirty river
    Zipped with zigzag lights
    Are shores where the stale tides
    Duly deliver
    Their dead-letter load of nameless junk.
    How sweet the moonlight sleeps upon this drunk.

    Factory chimneys patient and desolate
    Like treetrunks struck by lightning wait
    Their demolition in some foreknown time,
    To lie with daisies and disintegrate.
    Great Babylon's fallen, fallen
    And solemn flows the slime.

    Yet, in their hour of wealth and potence failing –
    The wallpaper peeling off the mantelpiece
    High up in a bombed site –
    Did Babylonians too delight
    In bridge and lamp and stair and railing,
    Even in the Almighty's threat that scrawled their ceiling?

    What if the fuse of death is fired
    At birth for every soul and town,
    Its burning snake is still desired
    And loops a charmed festoon
    From pole to pole of ticking nights,
    A children's dance of coloured lights.

Battersea Pleasure
(a visit to the 1951 Funfair in Battersea Park)

With a fanfare for the funfair
Step up the light fantastic stair!
Whip like a prize-top
Up to the sky's top
Whirled in the Great Wheel-chair,

Carefree like a firefly
Round the rococo spire fly,
Pineapple pinnacles
Plastered with barnacles,
Figures of intricate wireply;

Children's boats
Bump out from harbour
Underneath the candelabra,
Scenic obscenical vertigo-down trains
Plunge through rickety wickerwork mountains,

Battersea powerhouse chimneys throw
Their funny hats to the sunset glow
Playing giants for jacks below;
Silent Thames reflects to starboard
Canopies and cones and cardboard.

So by quaint contriving we
Conniving against gravity
Lost romantics
Choose our antiques
From Emett's missing century;

Pied John Piper curls our tune
Sculpting the marble-toothed lagoon;
Where its mercury stipples
With voluble ripples
A shame to curb those curves too soon,

Our dull super-ego
With echo and stucco
With tassel and globe shall be dandled to sleep,
Till with double-deck rhyming
We storm up the ninepin
Horizon and capture the mastodon keep.

Sleeping Aboard

On the sea's lake
No wrinkle but
The sun's last track,
Gone with glittering foot
Down an opal wake.

Over the warm sand
No ragged hand
Of wind or paw of storm
Rips the fished-out nets of calm
Off the outpost land.

Waves' million shoals
Like fire-eyed coals
Wink with purple shadows' lashes,
And where the foam's torn sash is
On either side the dark increases.

Green and magenta hulls
The ghosting yachts slip in to sleep,
Shuffle down to the boom and strip
White or flamboyant sails,
And anchor to the stars with naked tip.

Come home to the sea
Now the land's drowned.
Launch out in the dinghy and be
(Before the world's last tide has turned)
No longer found aground.

Phone Call to Pat

Oh Pat, the spring is fast by half a morning:
Let's take the train to Greece.
You're packed with blue sky mischief. Bury the cynic
Shells-deep in your pockets, doodling ship-tall stories
On the irresistible pavement sand.
Five minutes to the boat, have a chocolate sandwich?
By the sunburnt watch-stripe on your wrist, Time Is.
See where she booms, boom laid hard over, funnels emitting
Oil-drum lozenges of a sinister prophecy
To the secretive harbour, which has heard
All truths, all travellers' tales
Wash with soiled wisdom under the porthole inns.
Fellow conspirator, strap me into my knapsack,
Men were born free, but everywhere ...
Robinson Rousseau tickles your Cockney irrelevance
--Girl, but it's Friday still. Phone me tomorrow,
Gotta work now.--What a time we had us
Under the marsh stars
When the tent caved in and it was too warm to care,
When we swam with phosphorescent eel-tracks
Out to the patient-flapping Dolphin
Ready for her take-off into the lost evening
Past the gulled hulls of one-eyed sleepers ...
Beyond the last tongue of sand the sad-eyed lighthouse
Foretold a lapping mist.
Resignation has always dogged our holidays,
The worm in the bud of adventure, the worm of returning.
One trip we'll take the others with us,
All the whole crew of them,
A Noah's Ark-hold of our ever or once beloveds,
Then nothing to turn back for.
Gotta work now.

Hymn for Summer
(in time of peace)

He comes at night in the summer lightning
Out of the waves to the bathers' feet,
For a count of seconds and miles his frightening
Hand is over their heart beat.

He rains on the disshevelled city
And the windowpanes of years wash bright,
HIe drums into the leaves for pity
Of all things pavement-mortified.

He fills a day with his blue nothing,
Yet each of its small lives admires -
The glass wings creaking in the heather,
The shining telegraph wires.

He stands among the green-eyed players
In trees beside the garden stage,
He guides the candled punt of singers
Down the river's arching age.

Then of his patience with our petulance
Whose grass of joys can scorch so soon,
He folds for autumn the sky's petals,
The sunset leaf sends loitering down.

Xenos 2   **Wayside Refuge**

Remembering the summer
My winter hearth draw by:
Sparks to the ceiling's glimmer
From April driftwood fly.

Odysseus lagged in leafmould
Between twin olives lay,
Like embers the tired farmwife
Banks down to keep till day.

Lakeland
(to my brother)

When we were young,
You and I, over the hills and heather,
Young, and together
In an earth and heaven all our own:
There was no richer tone
Than wind-washed sky, no sweeter scent than grasses
Growing in the mountain passes
Soft grey and sun-warmed: there we went, alone,
You and I, no sound but silence, leaping,
And earth had no more weeping,
Life no better gift
Than being young.

Then oh then
The certain cure of all the ages' sorrow
Was a warm stone, a gleam
On the opposite slope, soon reached, clouds wafting up the valley;
Then there seemed no tomorrow
As we watched the lowland hazes rally,
As we washed our faces
In a stream
Cold and tiny; then was all forgotten
But holy places
Standing on top of the world beneath the sun,
Or hand in hand the races
When sheer joy broke into a run,
Then stood, breath held, seeing the marshes sodden
Far down, after the tide, lie stretched untrodden.

It comes no more; though you and I together
Should go again,
And smell the wind and feel the springing heather,
And the sky after the rain
Be bright as in our childhood, yet in vain
Tramping the moors, looking at each other,
And the far edge of the hills,
Seeking to capture, seeking to remember
How we felt, what we said, what it was that possessed us
When we were young, that is lost now we are grown,

And find not the old silence that should rest us,
That once unquestioningly was our own -
Now we have noisy minds, and hearts of bother,
And look before us and behind,
In vain, knowing all this, would we remember
That once there was a time when life was kind,
When lying on the heather, in the sunlight,
With no today, tomorrow, yesterday,
There was nothing in us but the wind and silence,
And nothing that we wished for was away.

Life's Other Kingdom

Sometimes they cross our busy street of days.
Curtains of self-possession we still snatch
Aside, to guess their turning; half unlatch
Our cosy brains' conclusions at their gaze.
We may not find them beautiful, yet they cast
Disturbing shadows: one has subtle hands,
And one with eager head humbly commands
Some kingdom of the future or the past.

They drift with empty pockets. Ours are full,
Yet their fierce grace outbids our charitable
Works. They explain no reasons, keep no rule
We keep, show love to none of us - yet shame
Our too small loves, which tease, cheat, envy them,
Poor kings of a time past or time to come.

To E. M. C.

No, Sally, I will not send you a C.V.
If it is not worth remembering the firefighters arriving silently by
moonlight
Then the wartime Ministry of Fuel is as dead as war.
Before that, school was a tightrope equivocation
Between Greek verbs and falling hopelessly in love,
If I may not include both, then neither;
And college was a First bought by skating on the Cherwell,
Then a near disaster bought by cosmic anxiety
For a sick planet -
Which among its worser deeds, has put my best work in the
w.p.b.
If what I spoke in that was evil,
Bear witness of it
(Those who are not Christ may quote him)
Do not celebrate my worse work instead
Surrendering to Gresham's Law.

A C.V. would record huge gaps at the places where I really spoke.

I was like one who walks towards the mountains,
Deceptive air made distance clear to view.
I had my rations for a half-day's journey
And Everest to do.

We who keep safely to the middle road,
Blinker our eyes for fear of visitations,
Blinder than Paul of Tarsus before sainthood
Can all the same applaud

Your rare rash souls; you who once stopped and listened;
You whose sweet faces lost their homeward view;
Who have passed from land to land unmapped strange-missioned
Waiting to learn what they must do.

Some go mad, some die not breaking silence,
Poets whose own flesh is all their tune,
They are mariners and mooncalves and musicians
Under some ancient debt or doom.

Our pains they plumb; they dive below sea-level
Of dreams we float on; all things possible
For us, are real for them, and being true
Must be forgiven; they make all things new.

Lord, grace their souls to guard those outposts
To which each steered his course alone,
That when at last I fall through dark unbounded
Their stars shall draw my stardust home.

*   *   *

Retrospect

Let's (conscious of pretence) walk down the hill
Of the droll past we shared; we can gently now
Consider it with compassion: how absurd
My love, your shocked recoil. Look, there's the brown
(Approached quickly down the slope), the gruff square building,
The steps, the much-handled door; how long ago
That was; too long – rather, I should say, enough
Ago to give perspective. How wise we are,
Patient, forgiving, mellowed. Shall we go in?
The stairs creak like old times. Notions I had
Still stretch invisible cobwebs; they might check
All but the impious (Rubbish). There, your view !
Remember? What relative things windows are;
Who sees from it now, and with what right? which is
The true view? We were young then, harsh. Perhaps
We had something we have lost. You would not remember,
But once on the next landing--once on the lawn
When laughter blew like a curtain--If we wait
Will a breaking-point reassemble? Will you again
Turn fierce, fine, terrible, distant? Somewhere here
I cannot see for tears. We should have left me
Unspied on. It was a mistake coming,
Quickly, let us go down again to the street
Before the door slams, before the door slams,
Oh God, now I remember, there does come next
The slamming of a door
Traps part of me in the past for ever.

Poetry Lesson
(after A. E. H.)

A reader with a lovely voice
Undid me, long ago.
Her wooing was not meant for me
But how was I to know.

This glorious planet spreads itself
Yet in my heart is woe:
The wooing is not meant for me,
As now I think I know.

Pax tecum

Of all the monstrous claims my poems laid upon you
The worst or best was this I never plainly said
That in some other nebula you could have loved me
And that you told me so before we ever met.

Mood, Tense, Voice

There is no ease with you. In my own mind
I stroke your arm, I arrest you, watch your face,
I catch your slightest mood when you are kind,
I tease you out of frowns: I know your ways.
Your subtlest shades of voice and tense I know -
In my own dreams: but where are you the while?
Oblivious how I prison you you go -
Oh where? And smile you if my image smile ?

And when I am with you, ah, there is no ease,
I am stretched on the rack by my quick heart's travail,
I cannot feel beyond my trembling knees,
Or understand your speaking. Changeling frail!
Or masked? I dare not shatter it, I quail
You are close beside me, and there is no ease.

Packing Dream

What have I left behind? There is something, surely.
This room is filled with books and ends of thread,
Papers piled high and dusty, only half seen.
I have looked all round. (Why are those flowers dead?)
Nothing of mine is here but that tangled skein.
Yet half my possessions, those best known, most used,
I seem to lack. Can it be I am sleeping?
- I remember now. They must be in your keeping.

When the face of you ín repose can blur my sight
And the sudden lift of your glance catch up my breath,
What is the use of saying I will write
Your name to outlast death?

I chase with wreaths of language, round, above
To ring you – and draw back an empty net.
And then I find you suddenly, and for love
Stand inarticulate

I am not fit, because I love you so,
To meet you on the far side of my face
And fit my face to hide this and that show
Only, which does no violence to the place
And time: I am not fit, because I love
So much the moment, to enjoy an hour,
Nor taste, when to my sense a scent's enough
To maze all thought and conscience overpower.
I break the rules. I break the rules. Because
I love you so, I hate myself too much,
And hate the mean, stale, cautious crust of use
My fifteen years have made me. Shedding that crutch
I face you naked with no words to say,
And loving so, go dark and mute away.

Long Sentence

If you must leave me to my thankless dreams
Whose poisoned sweetness has been my downfáll,
If my presumption fit for laughter seems
And my dumb question moves you not at all,
Why do you then not tell me all the truth?
Why do we still so cruelly pretend?
While I, all-doubting, burn away my youth
With hopes that you may sometime be my friend.

If once we might stand fearless face to face,
Reading each others' thought in steadfast eyes,
And you might take my hand, and say "Your place
Is elsewhere. Go, forget, and be more wise" -
But no, you cannot trust me, nor can I,
With any longer sentence than Goodbye.

Visitations

To what end do you come or are you sent?
Since plainly my shrunk shame still disobeys.
My crime of loving you to make repent?
Yet how should it grow fainter in those rays,
How night by night should I unlearn to long
For what you blind me with, even as you turn and are gone?

If you're all dark, why do true angels not
Guard me more safely? If you are some truth
I lie to living daily, why not meet
Me in daylight, so I could become your Ruth?
I cannot lift the weight of those dream-veils
To flit at your command on through the outer gales.

I do not want to lose you. I consent
To this possession. Do I wrong you so,
Summoning a footfall I could not invent
Along the stone-flagged maze of long ago?
Surely some third world joins our threads together
Who could not so confront in the sole brain of either.

My dreams roll-call their silent witnesses:
The round stair and the window with no view,
The hush of gardens by a watered place,
All incommunicable signs of you.
If there's no sense nor glory in our meeting,
Why do they bend and sway with secrets beyond keeping?

And when your eyes meet mine, why are they cold?
Sad for my waste of life and hope and time?
Even by that look I know them yours of old;
You judged me then; the more I longed to climb.
So will to banish love from love derives,
Which when thrust deepest down, then roots and grows and thrives.

Goodbye until tonight. Come robed or pale,
I will not miss you, though I stand until
The lamplight weakens and the stars grow stale,
To see you vanish round the hurrying hill.
Oh sometime bring some sign so past mistaking
That whether gain or loss, it breaks through dreams to waking!

This was not loneliness, not to have held
Joint balance with you on the knife-edge of thought,
Nor in the darkness of a silence caught
Your flash of essence - only to have felt
A causeless, impotent pity at your being,
Your burning on alone without my aid,
And had no courage to stretch forth the shade
Of my soul's wings, for fear you scorned it seeing:
But, when the rare, significant pattern links
All corners of all worlds in unity,
And music breaks upon forbidden things
Across the locked gates of eternity,
Then of that joy I must suppose in faith
You witness, or be lonely unto death.

No longer stays the music in the dome
When the tense finger falls and silences;
And there's no help in the rapt breathlessness
That reaches after and would draw it home
Redeemed from change; when once it dies aloft
Down the dim arches of the echoing height,
Its wake across the brain foams into night
And you are but a song, grown sudden soft.
My hand, that since touched hands I did not love,
Forgets the way you held it; from my eyes
Unlovely sequence blots your image out,
And my ears lose your music; you who move
My thrice embattled reason into rout
Faint underneath the minutes' ebbless rise.

The imagery of these poems reflects that the addressee was a musician.

Revisit, Hampstead Heath

Blame not these shadows for dissembling
If they the secret of the world refuse;
Say not to the leaves in autumn tumbling
They are phantoms of their former hues;

Think not the mists and pools of altered fashion
If now their beauty is not fathomless;
The loss that here becomes the thought's obsession
Is never loss of theirs.

If alien faces now by path and window
Pass, there's no help in conjuring back the old,
On them alike would fall the shadow,
Their changeling looks be to my question cold.

Then I'll not even anchor
My search on one for whose sole sake
The whole seemed beyond price, not any longer
Powerful to give me back what she had power to take.

Oh, I came seeking
A bloom on slopes of grass, a slant of trees,
A memory, even if not perhaps a meeting:
And I found these.

I nowhere found the old generous inspiration
To set all sails for beauty's reachless coast:
What use to search the earth and heaven,
It is myself that I have lost.

So I from fruitless visit
Turned back, and loss pursued
In shadows unexplicit
And leaves November-hued.

How can I alter what I am
When what I am you formed before I knew?
How can you find it in your heart to damn
This image drawn from you?

If I have copied wrong, it was from lack
Of time and grace and kindness;
If your dark side I throw you back
It is not just from blindness.

If I was wrong to copy, wrong to love,
Then you were wrong to be;
It was not possible you should not move
Me by your company.

And when we had to part, so cold, so soon,
It was not possible that I
Whom now you chide for blankness, should not lose
The light out of my sky.

Quicksands

Because you did not want my love
I gave you raspberries and cream
And washed my college curtains clean.

Because you did not want me by
I learnt to live with absentness
And let my inkwell hopes go dry.

You bade me not remember you
And so your image carved and true
I sank beneath the daylight's blue -

No, you cannot dredge my dreams.
Nor you nor I can thence retrieve
The hostage you were loth to give.

I have resigned all your bright lands;
'Ware searching then on my quicksands,
My thirsty sea has eager hands.

Your final word comes as no coming:
The blank road is a cypher plain,
The unwritten letter makes all known.

Without reproach, without remainder
By negatives I now complete
The strongest actual I have met.

Since in the crowd you do not wish
To know my face, your face goes by
Stared at and stolen instantly,

Exchange and motion both denied,
Frozen in my mirror to abide
As first I saw it truthful-eyed.

Without reproach you too must brook
The right I keep beyond revoke
To recollect a stranger's look.

You cannot cut the fine threads quite;
Unwilled, unwelcome though it be,
You once on me let fall your light.

Blot me out of your care and thought -
God never sets the past at naught:
I coined from you no counterfeit.

Onlie Begetter

Then be assured
You cannot so disown my sorrow's children,
Although I know I slept with you in sleep
Moon-raped Endymion,
You cannot so
Force me to feign with your fierce chastity
There was no issue of that hour;
When eyes lit with your image true
Pursue you through the woods of dream
You cannot give the lie to their sweet likeness
Nor your own self unseem
Against their recognition piteous-lipped;

Send me them back because they came unbidden,
But never say you never gave me aught
With that proud stare as of a face mistaken -
In the blank crowd they know
Your brow's lift with a leaping more than certain
That can strip from years the obliterating curtain,
Those children I stole off you long ago.

Oh love is not these waves, it is the tide
As all my crested hopes are dashed on earth,
And to the shapeless waste that gave them birth
Drag the spilled fragments back, from which has died
The inspiring form that bound the single whole,
It seems the end to me. Yet is not so.
From the spent spray some power I do not know
Welds a new surge to thunder through my soul.
Like sea and land we battle, you and I.
Water's an easy-wounded element.
Is altered, pierced, moved from its course by all
That touches it. The broken wavelets fall;
From their very death gathering power the sea
Advances its unquenchable intent.

I dreamt we lay in yesterday again:
Ordinary people, sharing a weekend
With shops and heat and bright punts along the bend,
And the mood when meanings flicker smooth and plain,
And suddenly you turned to me and said
"But why have you chased me through the seven heavens?"
And I said "Not for givings or receivings,
Only for this." And watched the stream ahead,
And knew for once on earth I did not care
What other hours or places lay outside,
And had no more stake in anything elsewhere.
"This empty-handed present is the peace
I lost in you, long since." You were satisfied,
And we strolled back through evening well at ease.

Password

I lay in bed and heard you playing. Notes
Flowed with the passage light beneath my door,
Peepholes of comfort in a world obscure.
Down tapering staircases through strange abodes
The tall chords led me, opening at each close
On dreamier distances of mirrored floor;
But yours the central room towards which I bore
Fled me. Oh held that mansion only ghosts?

My opposite wall with vaguer, vaster shine
Was keyboard to the hidden moon, which knew
My wonder hang on it no more than you.
And cared no more? Oh since I must sometime
Climb that remoter staircase, let me know
The taste of welcome here before I go!

Calm as a lake my mind
When the light's flown:
Your absence, a sole thought
Rippling the stillness evenimg wrought,
Sinks, like a stone.

Driven as a ship my soul,
Past reef and reef:
Your presence on the foam
With lamp of dawnnlight points me home
From the seas of grief.

Staying at Chart Sutton

This loyal worm to your tried tolerance, greetings.
No, but seriously: it hurts to admit
To a love more long than brave. Daresay you think me
Imprinted on you like a bloody duckling.
Whether is it easier to say "I forgive sins",
I see the perfect form behind the confusions of firelight,
Hear the indreamt chords across the divergent life-noise -
Or to rise up and walk, and make the morning tea?
But one must ache towards both. Therefore when I dream
Suddenly over the washing up, be charitable,
The timeless vision loomed a moment,
The dried year's petals shower'd on mé.
How can we lay the ghost between us two
Who is always there, who gives our meetings over-
And under-tangs of bittersweetness, who
Is dead, if the past can kill (and that's a never-
To be eased-of doubt) yet if she were here would
Drive you to exasperation, me to heart -
- Break wilth her impotent innocence, with her good
Gold good-for-nothing love, a sleeping partner
In all mere waking schemes, my vanished self:
With her wide sad eyes watching, empty now
Of disappointment, hope, perhaps all else
Too soon; if she had waited - can we know
Who it is still seems to wait? it is a cruel
Thing she should not share what I now enjoy
Grace to her patience: not have held this jewel
The meeting of our eyes - which we soon drop
With a timed seemliness, yet turned into
The darkness that engulfed her, might shine through.
Forgive me, that I cannot banish her.
It is hard for anyone to find a future
Who must pretend away the past.

Triad

The treble spikes of iris glimmer
Where three ways meet;
The three dimensions of the summer
Are wires alive with heat,
Beneath whose gauze the holy Trinity
Make veiled yet bright embrace -
Ah then why should our triangle of three
Ache without grace?

Him who desires me you desire
And not me who desire you;
Could we with grammar not conspire
To make these linking meanings flower
And so for ever snare you
And him and me sweet-bitter rose
In threefold tension of repose
And power?

But still the obscurest task must be
The gentle task of go-between,
Last godhead yet unrecognised,
Descending breath divine.
And so I without precedent
Between your opposite poles am bent
And launched at the dark future's chord
To implant the missing third of God.

Cupid's Rose-bed

Sleep, my sweet love, and let the night play on
With stars for harp-strings, beaming through your hair
To drown in lakes of silence, even where
My fingers drown, and travel as they drown
Through fronds softer than under ocean grown
Float from its wrinkling bed of sheeted sand.
This air, in which I stretch my lazy hand,
Sways with no tide, unless my pulse is one,
Yet we two lie like sunken treasure trove
Beneath diminished stars; and our limbs roll
With water's heaviness. Your touch on mine
Floats past and by, anchored no moment still,
Or trembling stops me like a violin;
Stop now, and on that last note sleep, my love.

Two Dreams
(after Blake)

There are two dreams in which I meet
The essence of all dreams discrete:
The sleek and silent snake that goes
About the garden of the rose,
The silent rose which in its core
Reveals the snake that was before.

The garden is of green and grass,
A grass that rustles as you pass,
The hedge is duly clipped and true,
And the pale rose against the yew
Is sweet to fondle, sweet to smell
And in its heart the coils of hell.

If the snake was before the rose,
Then all life down a tunnel goes.
If the rose was before the snake
Then life should never dare to wake,
But linger cradled in sweet breath
And be itself its own self's death.

But life, the evil thing and good,
Close-linked, entangling, through-and-throughed
In every petal with vile thread
Looks out, a petal-tongue-tipped head,
And who would either live or die
Must grasp this fair monstrosity.

So in my dreams I softly tread
The lawns of my enchantress dread:
If soft enough, I need not wake
The monster, nor the blossom shake,
Nor yet in the bud of time unhearse
The serpent-circled universe.

If the snake is a phallic symbol, the Garden of Eden story is a demographic theory of human ills. So to psychoanalyse this poem is to validate my demographic poems on pp 70 ff.

Wind-player

I love you best as good as gold,
And that is when most unaware
Of everything but what you hold,
The reed, the wood, the keys, a world
In which I am not there.

If I could have become some tool
Through which your curious nature spoke
Yet kept my sovereignty in cool
Collusion with our compound whole,
Both could embrace that yoke.

But souls with souls do not meet so:
The dreadful equals of their eyes
Both speaking, across silences
Through which till Judgment Come they go,
Their separateness know.

So I, who have by heart no tune
But what your eyes forbid me play,
Must there be taught to turn
My own best face away,
And learn, before I burn, some lonelier way.

Raindrop Prelude

The hooded trees of purple night
Stood close for blessing at your hands.
The wind that hardly stirred their weight
In you became swift eloquence.
Between two worlds the lawn was warm
Waiting for the coming storm.

The rain of music stirs no grass
Yet faint thirsts in it revive
Like the lime scent fugitive,
Everlasting while they last.
Between the garden doors the glade
Laid its listening paws of shade.

You closed the gleaming cedar cone;
Hands possessed their music still,
White gestures of caressing bone.
You crossed the garden and were gone.
Through the panes inscrutable
Outside the real rain began.

Different Dream

Stare out the ashes, let the hearth grow colder.
Our little sleep is rounded with a word.
Even as the winds of silence, blowing bolder
Had quickened in us too a smoulder,
And the key of your hand seemed to unlock my shoulder,
We saw the angel with the flaming sword.

That flame out-singes
This: therefore to bed,
Separately as we are separated
By all the laws which time has made.
The door of eternity swings back on its hinges:
Ours up the other stair must lead.

The beauty of your hand was worked in marble
That daybreak when even stones were soft
Beneath the newborn sun's creative gift.
Only who loves as warmly as God then loved
Might once be able
To melt your form back wholly and so be unrebuffed.

Men love a woman's softness, I her cold.
They choose her where she thaws most easily.
I choose in you the inmost gold,
Your heart yet my heartbreak I hold
Which as by them it cannot be despoiled
So never will by me.

They snatch a moment while the angel sleeps
Or turns his stifled face away.
I have looked straight into his dreadful deeps
Of eyes, and met the barrier of his lips,
And for the still watch over you he keeps
I love that angel grey.

Goodnight, sleep without dreams
Follow us each to bed.
I like you better as truth beyond my arms
Than phantom in my head.
So then, when daybreak comes
Nothing is lost that harms.

You shall remain my daydream. Though I learn
The hard way men call real (was yours less hard?
I have dreamed diamond cliffs that daunted sight
And woke me astonished): though I learn to turn
Estranging road-bends far from what shone bright
Yet was called darkness: though I now discard
The peace and the anguish for a whiter light,
I know nothing can utterly blot you out.
If I must find the magic in the fact
Before the fact in magic, it is a sign
Magic keeps better. Some day the world's doubt
When I have learnt the world's harsh tongue for mine
I'll quench with witness. Till that hour, the act
Is absolute, and the might-be is moonshine.

*   *   *

Against hero-worship

Nobody is all that important -
Lie in the grass, warm with the sky -
Small grains spin round larger grains
But even the largest are not self-stable,
Satellites all, we fly
Between poles that are non-existent
Turning, turning
With the grey willow leaves
Like trout in a stream, seals in a wave-trough,
Tumbling to the great wind of nonentity -
Trust it, bear your own weight
Bravely, do not lean too hard
On any leader, Christ, Shakespeare, even,
There is no centre that does not shift
Under the full weight of human craving -
Gravitation can kill
Lie lightly on the good grass of what you love,
Reserve always
Something of your own selfhood
To be borne without sharing
Creative or ignominious, sad, godlike.

Kenwood Concert

Above the lake-bound music
Where sunset mellows grey,
Beyond the lawn's tired people
Who watch the fiddlers play,
The massive beeches sway.

The planes and oaks and ashes,
Old as all forests are,
Remembering in their branches
Night-sounds remotely far,
Frame round our listening hour.

Joy, grief and calm we compass
In this rapt interlude;
The notes assail the leaf-mass
With human pulse and mood;
The leaves remain and brood.

Only their colour changes,
From green to gold to dark,
Through infinite gradations,
As though the beat they mark
Had all time for its arc.

They tower in trance and leisure;
Below, the tense hands play,
Who must plead out their pleasure,
Growth, glory and decay,
Before the close of day.

Titchfield Abbey

Five Kings made welcome here, and twice a Queen,
Built by an Earl whose grandson loved a poet,
My beauty is my past. My doves careen
Through stairless towers where Juliet first was seen,
And sightless mullions where the master wrote,
And keep a tryst unanswered, and bemoan it,

43

June Midnights
(translated from Victor Hugo)

In summer when the day has fled
          from plains that are knee-deep
In flowers, air like lavish wine
          both near and far is poured;
Thoughts barely slumber, ears incline
          to every sound abroad;
With eyes transparent on my bed
          I lie in a half-sleep.

The stars put on a purer dress,
          deeper the shadows twine,
Yet ghostly-light the vanished day
          still haunts the eternal dome,
And dawn, a presence soft and grey
          before her hour has come
Flickers all night in readiness
          along the low sky-line.

Anchorage

In drag-net stars we lay, and there was no
Cloud, wind or moon. The heat hung silently
Baffling the waves' lift. Over the sea came
A sail like ours, and vanished, as our boom
Swung to the changing tide, and brought up land
Remotely, with a lighthouse signalling
And one red eye that never blinked. My friend
Shunted trainloads of dreams. Too hot to dream,
Becalmed out of the pools where I would swim,
I planted the roots of my fingers in the stars,
Exploring for their bright anemones.
They would not budge. The tide, now singing fast,
Loosened my final star-clutch wavering,
And swept me down sleep's dark, all moorings cast.

Open Air Theatre
(Shakespeare in Regents Park)

The king has led his courtiers to the glade
(Poise leaf, pose flower, to frame their west-light faces);
The hero hides in cloak of puzzled shade:
Crowd to his undisguising, trunk and blade -
These of rich velvet, those with glittering bosses -
Sure Birnam woods are come to Dunsinane,
Trees move, and souls grow roots across the lawn.

He with tree-patience bears the storms of chaos
(Lance, level sun, these tanglings with calm light),
Till inward winter strips and whirls his joyous
Plumage of language down on his destroyers
To the last painful word-fall. We who wait
In silks and sunlight for June's gentler dark
Seek interval in the reassuring park.

The humming midge of story starts again.
We settle shawls, and wonder wanderingly
At here the shot-gold leaping of a faun
And there a proud eye's flash of archery;
Some Ariel with green eyebrows dazzles by,
Passionless, exalted, sprung from that high elm
To tease us with a scent of his rare home.

But finally the human hour returns:
The lady lights her candle of consent.
Droop leaf, drop flower, while that one window burns
Holding a stained glass handshake: and relent,
Gnarled hearts of thorn-bushes, which still defy,
Now conquering truth has furled its blazonry
The tailpiece of a smoke and ochre sky.

The Singer
(For Kathleen Ferrier)

She laid upon our waiting hush
The finger or her certainty,
And shaped our ragged past with woman's hands:
Come unto me, come unto me.

We stayed and sat in staid array:
And she it was who came -
Down every crimson staircasec running
Through the impassive dome.

She gave us roses from her dress:
Uncurled their hearts of careful gold
In each private wilderness
Crying Behold, behold.

Down balconies of hanging lights
Which shone on her white eager face
She launched the birds of her sunrise
To reach our cobwebbed place.

She led us where the wells of life
Still spring in pure and silver rain,
Whence whosoever's given to drink
Shall not thirst again.

*

After Bach's Magnificat

Great singing is the nearest thing to heaven I know:
The soaring arc, the blazing track across an ocean's flow,
The staunchless undertow
The immaculate ecstatic sunburst shapeliness
Et exultavit spiritus
Mother with child for all creators voicing
Perfection's justified rejoicing:
'Perfect' means brought to pass, to birth,
Delivering what was promised from the first dawn of earth ...

I wrote a second verse but deleted it; words can never equal music at its own game.

46

Chorus and Master
(For Reginald Jacques)

He moves like a stallion-figured barge,
And then like children on a shore
Stroking the seaweed. Studied more
His roughcast face is sad and large,
His polished hands embroider air
Or lance it more than surgeons' dare,
Yet anxious, as though life their charge.

His fingers curl the whips on sound
Whose glossy sheen from fiddles sprang,
And when the deep-hooved basses clang
He smiles, and bends to the rebound:
Now speed throbs through the air like foam,
Till a faint shuddering answers from
The sleeping giant in the ground.

Sleep far off, giant ocean's roar:
We'll play with him in a fringed pool
Of filtered sunlight over-full
That spills in rims on the bright shore;
Through his expectant fingers runs
The white sand of our myriad tones
And settles to the subterranean floor.

Where the grail shines and furls again
In secret rooms half-open, where
Bach's house of many mansions, stair
On climbing stair receives us in,
My home since home unsheltered me,
Times past and future dancing interchangeably,
You whom we love conduct us there.

Translation of *Um Mitternacht* by **Rückert**
(sung by Ferrier in Mahler's setting)

This midnight hour
I wake and stare
At the steep sky's pavilion;
No star from starbeams million
Laughs back from there
This midnight hour.

This midnight hour
My thoughts explore
The cage of darkness grappling:
No news of light their trampling
Brings me for cheer
This midnight hour.

This midnight hour
I bend my ear
To my own heartbeat pounding;
One drone of sorrow sounding
Is all I hear
This midnight hour.

This midnight hour
My arms I bear
For you, mankind in anguish;
Nor can contrive to vanquish
With all my power
This midnight hour.

This midnight hour
My utmost power
Into Thy hand is given,
Lord of the dead and living,
Thou watchest o'er
This midnight hour.

From a cycle of Orpheus poems I wrote in memory
of Kathleen Ferrier, who died of cancer aged 41.

The Set Apart

Their eyes are steadier than the flame
Of candles on a windless night,
Smiling yet sleep-walking bright.
A kindling crowns the hair of them
With unexplicit diadem,
They have no pride
Save that of the high dark towards which they ride.

The shafts of envy press them round,
Then meeting what their faces hold
Flinch away and fall to ground.
They are not self-enrolled.
They were in divers places found
Playing along the daybreak shore of the world
Till fetched by the great sound.

And he of these by his sad grace,
His pulsing hands and violet breath
Could be known surely, and confessed
Strange intimacy, when he played
The scrawled signature tune of death.
Yet not till we received his kiss
Did we believe he must keep faith.

Where she is gone and he must follow
The silver defile glimmers down,
Through which the immortal marchers hollow
The ancient heart of stone.
The marchers heard his flute of sorrows
No other toil but theirs could solace;
They know their own, they know their own.

Flute is a reference to Gluck's D Minor flute solo

Eurydice
("O röschen rot")

If then she was the soul beyond his singing,
What more is known? since what is far is far
Always,and why should there
Be more to a gold sound than meets the air?
A crest, a ripple in the stuff of nothing,
A wave which no-one waves in recognition,
Though rainbowed with the speed of light's desire.

If she is true and he has looked upon her
Even once, that one time is the whole of times.
Behind the glass walls there is then encounter,
And lives are more than names.
Oh you rose name, we cannot hold
That when we unrobe you fold on fold
There's nothing left but the dust scent of gold.

*

Was she a story or a soul?
God's game with her worked out so clear
With symmetries for his great ear
Who crucifies the part to whole.

My spinning discs of memory
Down years of dust undimmed have sped,
Touch of a switch still readmits
To her cathedral head.

But ah, remind me, lest my ears
Confuse remembered joys with heard
That I cage here a vanished bird.

The Hem

("If I may but touch the hem of his garment I shall be whole")

How close is touch? Nights know how far
Lovers embraced can part in mind
And one star miss another star.

I scud the human surge behind
Bleeding with light-years' loneliness
And grasp at garments in the press.

Dead poets' leaves - how close is touch?
Musicians' hands, whose eyes are blind -
How much communion is in such?

That virtue once left home in them
I cannot doubt, it burns my palm,
But how far back, from coal to flame?

Stars can blow out while their beams spread
Through universes in the dark
(How close is touch?) the news that they are dead.

They whirled out virtues from their thrum
Of carolling spheres, their firework's arc -
Spilt coppers for the halt and dumb.

And I stand thankless in the dust
They left, and seem not yet uncursed
Till one turns round to ask who touched.

Auditor

A woman there alone. Her unloved face
Turns down the mouth corners; bejewelled eyes
Demand the next sop without joy. The food
Is music. She's no doubt the love is there
(No fool), she sees it, in the runneled grace
Of hands, receives it in the turbulent air
(Two senses geared to distance), gladly would
Smell, taste, touch such refined delicacies
For ever. But she never smiles. The sense
(Like sight) of hearing feeds on absent things.
The two black-suited men on the platform are
Lovers. She knows that. Such circumference
Implies a centre, a true presence? Ah
Fool, sister - touch alsó stops at the rims.

Aldeburgh

Associate with this spine of land,
Of shingle dwindling to a long hooked tail,
All things that defy formlessness, and stand
Foursquare against what bids them fail,
Stout walls, two streets in parallel
Offering a self-sufficient front
Church, Moot House, lifeboat, concert hall,
From whose neat phalanx none would know
The sea holds half the town below.

Maestro
(For B. B.)

Famed, praised, envied, adored, they'll celebrate him.
Which of course are not the point. His works came first,
These after. He grew to the measure of his fame,
One sees, chosen not choosing: by a gift
Earlier than goodness, a quirk of genes; became
By vast routes worthy of his start. He must
Have toyed at times with loneliness, with the road
Of self-despair - he tells of it: so wide
The gulf he had to uncross, between the world
And his doomed natural platform. If in the end
He walked its grace ungrudged, performed his station,
Found in its eminence lost normality
Of being in the open what the witches made him,
Perhaps that proves he loved us; wanted to be
Among us, even on those terms, even solitary.

Tenor with Horn

I in a horn-lit glade once overheard
While undertones from the busy scrub were piping
And the curled heads of stags went silently stepping
A hunted and a huntsman that in one song concurred.

Too late for morning were the spiked ice stars
And all in a grey dew fell to the grass,
And where the huntsman and the stags did pass
Dazzled the world like cornices of glass.

Then took the hunstman his curled horn and blew.
And all the high-stepping creatures suddenly stood
And in their arching glory two by two
Ringed round that shape of Orpheus in the wood.

Lord, through the flight and pain of all live things
Above man's greed lightening thy sunrise wings
Conscript his ah! self-seeking eloquence
To join the music-makers and the saints

Festive

I am young enough to imagine the perfect company,
Old enough to know it folly.
He or she, both of them, or one or the other
Closes the poetry book, opens deep eyes on the foam,
Dives in, is versed in sea, I follow;
Then landfall joins us
Loitering-among sea poppy and sea lupin where the fine grass
Waves tufts of wellbeing,
Each of us figures in a landscape,
Praising through mutual silence
Which words only collude with.
Then home to the lengthening evening
And food in fresh season,
Till the pagan focus of the natural world
Contracts to our humanness,
A less impartial mystery.
I grew up in a dying world
Where persons talked and loved, not bodies grasped and rutted.
It has bright ashes. I would not outlast them.
Stir the log fire to a festive scent:
Tomorrow will be blue again.
How hard the myth of heaven dies.

O quietly pouring sea, offering libation
Over and over to a god of sorrows
Wiped away; sea of wishful peace, whose turning,
Like Dantean stars', wells from desire
For the high fixity, its rolling from
The goal of levelness, valleys exalted
And crooked straight - oh sea whose law of movement
Deduced itself from stillness, make me know
The same reconciliation, understand
There is no loss of hope in your for ever
Yielding, no fatigue of Sisyphus
In each wave's priming and collapse. I know
The sea triumphant even while I fear
Its wastefulness. Oh for such communion
With weather gold or iron, with the sun's and moon's
Scorching or blanching finger, with the hours
Of the brooding dove, the mood of journey's end
In every mid-sea Nowhere. So the albatross
Rests on its wings, and so said Keats a man's
Heart on his friends'. So rests
The turning globe on empty space
The elephant on the tortoise, in divine
Yet (trust) uncruel comedy.

It is my landward walk that has no prospects.

Burnt Concert hall

Musicians are active,
Audiences passive -
Musicians play, with art,
Audiences pay, with purses.
Players must work,
Listeners must weep.
Players earn proper pride,
Listeners learn sometimes self-contempt.
In any crisis,
A burst string, a missing part,
A burnt down hall,
Musicians with fire-fighting hands
Rise to the occasion,
Audiences sit to it, gaping.
And I wish I could break the order of nature,
I wish the sounds of others so long cherished in my head
Like a pregnancy never brought to parturition
Would break forth like song
And build a new heaven or roof and a new floor
And walls and windows
As a visible present for my beloveds,
So musicians could play
In my objective heart.
For who has not despised that place
While it held only privacy?

Wax Angel: a present from my sister
(in memory of K. F.)

She stands on the piano you lent me, among the china and violets
With a glass snake beside her and a reflection
Of her gold skirts in the mahogany, my paper
Angel, while she plays
Her toneless fiddle.
 (You and I have always shared
Music. The piano misses
Your lovely touch).
She has tinsel wings and a face of earnest sweetness,
And a halo which only half transforms
Her ball dress, her concert platform dress
Into the sad perfection that is worn in heaven.
She was made in Germany
Where they are not afraid to be sentimental,
And she stands for a singer some time dead
Whom I loved, while she lived, from a greater distance than
                              Germany.
She stands there not playing her fiddle
With her cheek tipped gravely sideways.

And I think that all people should wear the habits of angels
And divide gold strands of sound, and become as lovable
As those who are divided from us
By admiration and death,
Standing on platforms a little higher than knowledge.

For all musicians

The Pied Piper

(extracts from a long poem in which the Pied Piper leads
the children back again to rescue the adult world)

The Pied Piper leaned
His silver elbows
On his emerald knees
Pointedly, he sat
On his little canvas stool
Raking the roomful
Of expectancy and surprise
With his dark eyes
Travelling among their rows like heads of corn.
He laughed - then stopped
Looked fierce - looked fond of them
He said
'Dear follow-fellows'
(He had a thing like a stutter) -
And then some preliminaries which they didn't notice
Because with astonishment
They were registering
That on the yellow baldrick under his black cape
The silver flute hung,
Instead of the plain one,
The wooden for every day
Which they could all play.
Among many memories bright as glass
Through which that ever-noonlight shone
This one
Was rusty, ached when it turned
Like a forgotten key
In a locked piano.
Would he actually play it?
They were almost frightened,
Almost as if he were a cruel schoolmaster
Who usually inflicted a wooden rod
And today had a steel one.
But he didn't touch it, yet.
He sat and looked at them.

'The return expedition
Was bound to come'
He said.

*

His fingers
Were fidgeting ...
His face like a baby tortoise
Narrowed to meet the flute
Hard lips to nape -
He had thrown off his black cape
With its ground-length silver sleeve-linings
His D.Mus. for teaching purposes,
And in his emerald birthday garment
Glistened before them
A lizard, a freak curvature of light
In nature's four-square pane,
A wave, a wizard catspaw rifling
Their green depths
Into troubled seas
Or poplar trees whose leaves undress
Stripped upwards, they the electric sparks
He the silk wind,
Or God's good snake whose guile is grace
Not hatched till now - he double-tongued
To and fro on the narrow platform
Snake-hipped, like waterweed fighting a current,
Till their bright glass aquarium
Of desks caved in about them,
Tugged, wavered, slithered away downstream
And the flute's tide-race won.

I have not told you
What he played,
Or you who heard
Would not have stayed,
You my whole audience would be gone
To do what time needs done.

*　　*　　*

59

How blithe I dropped by parachute on Cambridge,
Neat baby spy assigned a rosebud lawn.
Five poplars barred the moon
That night of seine-net entry,
My one-way tunnel.

Such unfair luck I had,
Cushy quarters and ample dinners,
Innocent wavelenghts of unworldly thoughts
From parent scholars,
Beautiful sights and faces to surround me -
If part of it was mirage
Deserve the oasis part, oh you!
Safety of knowing
The others in the network too ...

How can this privileged person claim
To have been a hunted agent in a hostile land
Cassandra Mark Two version
"Still on the run" ?
Such ingratitude
Sometimes to have tested
Whether there was a way of twisting back
And found the seine-net disallows it.

Oxford Reunion
(unrhymed sonnet)

There was a hint of autumn all that day
In spite of broad July. The sun flowed full
Yet over-gently, with a whitening sigh
Among the discoloured leaves. Beside the river
All things of afternoon converged together:
College reunion, lawns of middle age
And the dowdy grandeur of the peonies.
We had achieved some honour, and this pause
Acclaimed us; we were dressed in summer shade
Prospering coolly. If the nights grew longer
They stole no waking hours yet. We were far
From times when the scant brazier of the midday
Scarce warms the hands of four o'clock, and after
The white snow shawls away both past and future.

Lament for an Oxford First
(with apologies to Wordsworth)

No notions has she now, no friends,
She neither knows nor cares,
Financed by earth's diurnal trends
In stocks and shares.

Distance at Christmas

One gulf is like another gulf.
The dead are not more far away
Than people that I know and lack
This Christmas Day.

If there is junction in the void,
All parallels must touch at last.
If none, then lovers in one bed
Asunder starve.

The motorways are ribbed with ice
And I must eat my feast alone,
And hear my records, like a long
Unanswered-ringing phone.

Why get the engineers called out
From Turkey, to repair the lines?
Communication is snarled up
By more than ringing miles.

My lines were always crossed, unclear,
The speech of love came scrambled thick.
I hear a little - grace for that:
That I am heard, I cannot think.

Yet those who living dared to call
Their songs across galactic space
Must have believed no solitude
Too deep for grace.

Open House

How it should be and how it is.
I keep open house here
For the mice and the dustbin men
Who remember each Thursday,
Touchingly, that there is this place.
I will myself to be more than caretaker,
Yet my thoughts fall like dustsheets
On the largely unused trappings
Carefully chosen, but
I do not need twelve chairs
Five tables
Seven beds, counting the Put-U-ups.
Oh greedy -
Well, but these things are for my heirs,
I am trying to hurry up and leave them.
Somewhere there is a planet
Petalled up secretly in the millefeuille recesses of the cosmos
Where this house serves the purpose of many mansions
Everyone I love has a room here
And there is no more death
Wages of sin, of the dialogue-busting faculty for increasing
                                    mutual distaste
As one gets older.

Amnesia

It's nice to know what one's looking for
My handbag, my dead mother, the name of that book,
Yesterday, forgiveness, the tea caddy
The vividness of my senses, when Spring
Was my spring, I heard higher than the lark
Saw sharper than the dropped needles of the sun.
Now even a stamp or a thought loses itself on the way across
                                    my room.

Incredibly, in big cities,
Booted aside, not fed, sleeping rough
Eluding the planning regulations
Unheard of by the Welfare

Under the feet of gardeners, dodging ashbin men,
Snubbed to the wall by all self-judged higher forms of life,
Having learned from long adversity
To erect spines against the hostile world

Lives, breeds, suns himself,
Survives, the hedgehog.
Hedgehog, I have a fellow feeling.
Lucky perhaps, if I too curl asleep some winter
Before the last penny's used in the gas meter.

Market-place

I have had my goods on the market stall
All day
Now it is evening
I will take them away.

Ring up No Sale
To the glum crowds
And slot back my tray of precious things
Into the little van their charnel-house.

Strangenesses and curios
Of a whole life: no takers.
Next stall for butterflies with pull-off wings
And cocktail shakers.

Riding a bicycle
Nose close to the ground
One sees the detailed entrails
Caused by the motorist
But beneath his notice.

Child rabbit
Mouth in his haunches
Squeals without organs
The throat's brakes jammed in vain
Tyres cleaned themselves of him

Nose that worked tasty wonders
Choosing grass differences
Now inedibly rubber-stamped on;
Hare's great ears uselessly attentive
Loll from the body's soup,

Hedgehog longing to curl up
Is pegged out flat
Pointless exhibit,
Mole meekly furred to the chin for its private occasions
Gets treason's quartering,

A puff-ball of once wren
Tiny flamboyance snubbed to a halt
By man's overruling dullness
So rudely forced
Tereu, tereu -

Dead lumps don't signify.
Yet I carry you home in my mind's bicycle basket
Dropping your small blood of tears behind us,
For I too belong among the snubbed ones.

(This poem explains the end of p.106)

My Gerbils

Everything to do with life
Is antinomous to dead things.
Mouse-war has begun -
Gently insidious,
All my inert belongings
Succumb to a film of fine sand -
Or do I now first see them truly?
Came into my life, came into my warm room
Two desert-mice with bluebird eyes
And a habit of hesitation,
Industrious flick-tails -
Do not misunderstand me, they are not slovenly,
They themselves always bud through with coats shining,
They are just continuously active,
Yesterday for them is a detritus
To be flicked to Kingdom Come.
So all my historied layers of past
Begin to get the burial dead things deserve:
Sand in my books,
Sand in this typewriter,
Sand, I suspect, winnowing beneath five lids
Into the holy of holies -
Lay not up treasures of canned music,
Dead singers cannot clear their throats,
My sand-frogs would not understand
Tastes that need dusting,
Joys that are at second-hand ...
How to live gleefully in a desert,
Since unto dust must all discs come.

Schoolmarm

You can understand this all of you.
This is teacher's English from a teaching type.
I have got you for an hour, for my sins,
For sixty pages of minutes,
I am nervous
I am as you see a nervous person
Twitch my skirt down,
Bothered about my hair,
Marginal note about terrible self-consciousness of women
Cressida Act II "we", "our sex", etc.
What play are we reading, Jennifer?
(What If, now I am rightly
Frightened, If this is a dream play,
No fixed lesson,
And something is turning over whose pages will bring
A terrible discomposing denouement
Too late to save you children
I mean me
From it).

I don't love you at all
You sit there in buttons and hair-ribbons
Expecting us to be boring
Mutually, I you, you me,
And the expectation of boredom is instead of love.
Write that on the blackboard, Philthea:
The expectation of boredom is instead of love.
You spotty little girl.

I have got you for an
Hour off eternity, hour of resignation
All our lives will be made up of hours
This is a sample,
From the cross-section you can see
In microcosm the soul laid bare.
Write that on the blackboard too.

*This is empathy with teachers I have known rather than autobiography; I
only taught school for a year when I was very young.*

What is English about, up to?
You think something little,
You try to keep it little, you write down always less than you are,
Self-belittling feminine, or is it self-greedy
You do not want to expend yourselves.
I am paid to expend -
But only for an hour
I am also grudging.
What if this present were the world's last night?
That Faustus may repent and save his soul.
Act V: one bare hower.

*

Apple Tree

Petals expendable
Cascade
    through sun and shade,
Not one by the warm
Transforming earth mislaid.

All I have thought and felt
Falls on what soil?
What conservation law
Redeems from spoil?

My animal being gladdens me:
My human being is not glad.
She-animal, part
Of all that breathes and shines,
With a warm core like earth's
And branching limbs,
And senses exquisitely savouring
The invisible shared boundaries,
Welcomed by all that is not self
As by a home with hands,
Rejoices;

She human, sad
At boundaries which exclude, exclude,
Invisibly tabooed,
Links with the oppressed great She, the earth
Ostracised from male sunship
And in self-darkness groping
As in the tunnels of a mine,
Where tears stemmed up for centuries
Seek junctions with all other blocked despairs -
Know, earth is truly Mother
Though her face concrete-plastered by man's works,
Until at last the outbursting of her grief
Alter the face of the land for good.

*

It is only to be expected
That the things thought by a maiden aunt
Should be too strong meat for organisation man
With his timid horror of not conforming.

Cassandra Passes

In a quiet voice
As if thinking aloud,
Muttering privately in public -
Arrestable almost,
A girl freak
As in Aeschylus
"I see blood on your shirt
You are guilty of a blood smell
Your eyes are withering lasers
What is there in that briefcase?
Open it policeman
I hear ticking!"
The gentleman's briefcase is perfectly respectable
The girl is off her nut.

Earth No Goddess

Mother, mother, mother
You no longer help me
The tax man has got me
The torture man has got me
There's sewage in my glass of water
Strontium in my food
Mother where are you?
The sea is poisoned
The air is all noise
The fields are cars
Father is arranging everything for the best
Mother I want to die.
When I was a child you were good and there
You took care of the world
Now the world is modern it has never heard of you
Mother, you are a lost continent, a lost earth.

Go Lightly
(March 1980)

The Sun is in his heaven,
The Spring draws on apace,
There's deep shelter in Whitehall
And calm in Portland Place,
We've planned our Home Defences,
And spent ten bob per head,
And England is Expecting
Her thirty million dead.

The current cost of burial
Is several hundred pound?
Well, let's not add up that one,
There wouldn't be the ground.
This is a crowded island
Fate planted in the way,
Which can't expect compunction
From super-powers at bay.

Lemmings will swim to drown them
When a birth-rate problem lours;
Rabbits can reabsorb them,
A trick worth two of ours.
It's hard to see what earthly
Advantage can derive
From thirty million murders,
Save fewer folks alive.

So here's a far, far better
Alternative, to wit
That every second person
Should volunteer to quit -
Anticipate the action
Of all that weaponry,
And keep our green and pleasant land
Still radiation-free.

Bequeathing crops to Russia
And oil to U.S.A.,
Our suicidal squadrons
Would earn a death-bed say:
Since people for a country
Are often called to die,
Accept our thirty millions,
But spare land, sea and sky.

*

Limerick

Please don't spin me this nuclear fable!
When bombs fall, I'll get under my table.
    If they kill one in two
    That deserves to be you,
Since your protests have proved you unstable.

*

After Omar

There was a dread to which man found no key:
A mushroom cloud past which he could not see:
Some little homes he had neath tree and sky
Awhile – and then no more of sky or tree.

Shore Scene with Plastic Cup

Little defilement
Where only wildness was,
You pop up crackling and grinning
Your split lip no improvement,
A cloud the size of a man's hand,
Whose predatory talons
Grasp at the sky.

I bend to pick the yellow sea poppy -
Oil-stained gash bleeds back
From glass not grass;
I plunge for refuge into the bracken,
Blue plastic fertiliser sacks
Deputise for the harebells
Indestructible, dead blue all seasons.

Homo sapiens deposits
Not animal droppings, that
The shore could use -
Excrement of the soul,
In idiot vanity declaring
Let all things vanish except me and mine
I am the only life worth having.

One day creation
Will take him at his dreadful word:
The sun fume-sickened flee
The sea boil tar-bubbles
The trees collapse like packs of cards
The billion genera and species
One by one lose heart -

Man's last temptation
To make a poem of an eyesore,
Forgetting sore eyes close;
Content to label
The obscene scrapyard
Neatly
"Police aware".

Biodiversity

("the earth is thronged
By man's oppression, and the poor worm doth die for't."
Shakespeare, *Pericles*)

In Paradise, that lovely land
God send the creatures to be named:
Bear, caterpillar, tulip, oak,
Jaguar, jacaranda, lime,
Seal, globe-flower, lark
In the rosy dawn of time.

How stands the long trusteeship now?
What roll-call write?
Adam, Adam, Adam, Adam,
Adam, Adam, Adam, Adam,
Eve, Eve, Eve, Eve
Eve Eve ... and then the night.

I know a secret which could save mankind,
How not to breed: short-circuit at the quick
The idiot optimist clamouring in the thighs.
I do not think mankind will learn my trick.

Moritura saluto

Lukewarm thanks for your hospitality, man's world.
You have fed and clothed and housed me.
I wonder why.

For anything I was
Or thought or felt or did, you cared as little
As if I had been born on Bettelgeuz.

I have not been one of your outcasts
Turned from the door by dogs
With no shift left but to curse you,

For that I have small excuse
Cursing takes heat
And our mutual dealings could spark no melt-down.

Oh you gave me a first class education
As they dress all the cricket team alike
Not intending the twelfth man should ever play.

You taught me language, and my profit on't
Is, I know how to do crossword puzzles.
There are a lot of different ways of being unemployed.

I am still Cassandra hunted through your dull landscape,
Tramp, prisoner escaping
Through your frozen heartlands

I carry my own snailshell with me
Living in its private blackout
Until boots crush the patterned shell.

A crowded world did not need my children,
An over-staffed world my scheming thoughts
An over-electric world my positive charges

Of sensual joy. (That may surprise you,
But you actually prefer good button-stitchers).
Women are for making carbon copies

And I needed to love from selfhood
Not from type.
On some other planet... - but that was a dream I had.

What I cared most about you ruined
Sea, sky, air, green land
Green water, litterless shores

The integrity of the sentient being.
Oh, I loved your musicians; but even they
Were not above cutting bits off boys for the sound effect.

Run your dark shambles
What you do you must suffer
I am outside.

I leave you to your dirty sea,
Your gutted lands. with topsoil gone,
Your own enormous progeny -
It would be weary to stay on.
My sex not formed to interfere
Your interference fills with grief
Man's world, man's world, I am glad to leave.

*

Mother Earth is a little dead fox
Whose brush hangs on the wall of a thousand board-rooms.
They still sit planning to hunt her
Haven't noticed
Dead fox into live lady won't go any more.

Hell Hellas: a Collage
(written during the Pappadopoulos regime.)

"The pursuit of wisdom
(Twist off his balls)
Is the greatest good in life,

I shall not be persuaded to refrain from it, fellow citizens"
(Make him eat shit
Choke him in his own sick)

"Bios anexetastos ou biotos"
The uninterrogated life is not worth living -
Place the electrodes

"Think again, Apollodorus".
The doctors in white coats
Attending closely

With all the accoutrements of healing
Sworn by Hippocrates
"Good sirs, consider"

(The man with the hemlock hung his head)

Switch on the current
Jerk scream jerk
Scream jerk scream

"We are lovers of beauty with due calculation,
And lovers of wisdom without loss of manliness".
Apollodorus blubbered

When the cup came for Socrates,
His own loss abjectmost.
"Was it for this that I sent away the women

(Having built my commonwealth epicene),
That my death-hour might be seemly,
Souls exchanging thoughts in a quiet room"

Not feet beaten like fillet steaks
And under the grill they go
What is live flesh but a smell of burning

Mutely ascending to the tourist altars -
Obscene city
Once so proud that all Barbaria

Built on her model.
The ritual road leads still
Downhill from humanhood and godhead

In the name of the Father and of the Son and of the Parthenon
I inject you screaming mad
I ignite these faggots

But he spoke of the temple of his body.

                              *

People have been gloating over the crucifix for 2,000 years
And they haven't got any less cruel.
I think Christ would like them to put it away now,
And lift up their eyes to some less obscene reminder.

                    *   *   *

I have learned to hate
Time for my death has come.
One thing I never knew
When I was young.

Weather

Something mankind has done has killed the spring.
My childhood March was glades of daffodils
Beneath new diamond birch-leaves glittering,
Soft mild-eyed skies; Chaucerian Aprills
Sweet never cruel; warmth that climbed like sap
Mercurial to the blaze of Mays. But since,
May sulks a lead-lid iron age, tooth-gapped
With backward trees. Do Jets disjoint the winds,
A bone-ache from the North avenge the poles
Melted by lusts of commerce? Seasons retard
Like seabirds oil-fouled. - Then, three children played
As though our acre jewelled the milk ring
Of teatime stars, our nursery homed All Souls.
Something mankind has done has killed the spring.

'You must be patient, Uncle Vanya, you must be patient'

There is no need -
Though the sun's hand spreads waiting,
Though clouds blow up with sudden threats,
Though the tides of the moon through the leaves' black sails
                    run racing,
Though the rain's disconsolate invitation
Against your winter window frets,
There is no need
For either deed or passion.

It can be learnt
That night's and day's procession
Piles towards no pagan temple's rite
Beyond the initiate hills' intense horizon,
And to miss that moment is no mission
Betrayed nor God left crucified -
It can be learnt
Skies want no intercession.

Others can meet
A human face and not imagine
The searchlight worlds all beamed one way,
Or know that glow is only a trick of the staging,
Not the rose dawn of revelation
Or lightning stroke of judgment day;
Others can meet
And part without distraction.

There is no call
In the sound of steps on a pavement
To run behind and spell some warning
That will blast the housetop hordes with a single statement,
And send them running for dispensation
From astral wrath with street-full mourning;
There is no call
To scald and scatter abroad a nation.

Let well alone.
Things grew without your action.
They will not falter when you grow tired,
Will not lose heart from failure of your compassion,
Will not lose flame or flight when your stationed
And cónfined brain seems no longer fired.
Let well alone,
Be shown you must be patient.

Bluebell Wood

Where beech-vaults fanned and lit
The April mist of it
This morning I went through
And through the bluebell wood
More and more thirsting for
Their hue of water blue
Their cry of fallen sky
Their lakes of distance beneath climbing columns
        Of warm grey somnolence
        Uplifting frailest wafer greens
        To the benign sunshine
        That sifted bright all shifts of shade -
Trees to themselves
Beneath their huge protectors
The bluebells grew and grew,
In congregations stood
And jostling swathes from near to furtherest blur
Of absolute blue
As I went through the wood.

Midwinter Snow

Startled out of absorption
Stone rabbit bunches hurly-burly
Towards igloo warmth;
Pernickety bronze pheasant

Chooses a route. Think of the hedgehog
Lucky perhaps in a last sweet meal,
Curled in spine-deep trance.
The electric squirrel

Poises like a chemist's balance.
The puffed birds slow with cold
Have each coal eye banked up
To last till morning.

The mad starlings
Wheel in two great flails, winnowing the sunset,
Split-second interlocking,
No hierarchy but absolute dance

It is dark already.
A million sparks of consciousness
Twinkle the winter land
Each its own Bethlehem.

Penniless eaters, coatless sleepers,
To whom my dreaded worst is comfort,
Escort me, fragile populace
Through night's and winter's wood.

The Frozen Lake

"Tell me, where have you been?
Come and sit by your mother
Where the velvet cushions smother
The lamp's bizarre mosaic.
Have you been out in the snow
And picked up a blackened stick by the frozen lake?
Is it there you have been?"
"No."

"Have you brought back a souvenir of your journey?
Saved me an apple of Paradise
(Since I for you once paid much price)?
Or a Dead Sea Apple which I could share
As I once shared the grief of your broken plaything?
What is it you bear?"
"Nothing."

"Well, if far lands bore you no fruit,
Tell me the tale of the travelled miles;
Out of successful ordeals told
Weave me a shawl to keep out the cold;
Only one moment of these long years rehearse
For which you have left me alone."
"There were none.
It is I who was the lonely one."

"Why, but you have been in my thoughts
All the time, and in my compassion.
Have I not in yours?
You have been with me here in the house, my son, my daughter,
Have not I come out of doors?
I would follow your footsteps wherever they have been,
Therefore spread the map on the floor and point with a pin."

"Oh mother cease
Your questioning dread
Leave things not to be borne
Unsaid.
I have been in a land
Where you were not
And this you cannot
Understand."

My mother thought me wonderful,
She stroked me on the head
There was no-one else in all the world
As nice as me, she almost said.

She lied. Six thousand millions' right
Against my own is hurled
Who day and night for the title fight
Of nicest in the world.

They work for me, I work for them,
They build with stones I hew,
I eat the bread they reap, but yet
I never get my due.

Is this world fair? oh, just and fair
But that's to share with all;
But when shall I that fairest wear
Which crowns me imperial?

Then in their ranks I ghastly see
My own thrice private mother
Competing for the crown with me
Or giving it to another.

Christ Jesus heal my loneliness.
Yet why for thee do I pine?
Thou lov'st six thousand million souls
As much as mine.

What should I believe?

Well, all creeds include the incredible.
What about the Russian dolls of mechanist biology?
Inside each automatic pilot, another automatic pilot.
What could be the point of that?

Admetus

I am Admetus
Who swapped my wife for life.

Life is duly obliging me.
I have lunched on fresh shrimps
They were not even expensive.

The July sun amazes the roses
To unheard of scentfulness;
The universe is triumphant about something

But if that is a victory over death
I am somehow not on the winning
Side I bargained for.

My skin is caressed by the soft wind.
So what.
Oh, I am not anxious, I am not in pain

But then neither should I be if I were dead.

"May all your pleasures be solitary ones"
Her eyes said
Leaving me, as I had chosen.

Couple

The thing they made is broken
As all things break in the end,
The vows un-spoken
And the rifts past mend.

Human unkindness is
A bottomless pit
Unnoticed as
We fall in it.

The first poem is Euripides' version of the story, in which Admetus readily accepts at first his wife's sacrifice.

Robbers of the Past

There is a kind of robbery more horrible than a sawn-off shotgun,
Than body-snatchers, who turn up a beautiful face worm-white at
midnight,
More excommunicative than the Paradise-gate sword,
So that the rifled heart after its long slow treasure-building
Has nowhere to go when it dies.
"Of course I played with you as a boy, but who else had I?"
"We always knew it was just conceit in you,
That labouring up the hill of heavenly truth."
"One has to be honest, admit it was my double vision
Made me ever suppose the woman I love sat in your shoes."
Robbers, robbers of the one place that is past reach of help:
Even God cannot remake past time -
But they can.
"Then I saw there was a way to hell even from the Gates of heaven"
The biggest snake after the topmost ladder.

Ichabod

From scarves of gold and blue to fire-panic broadcast overhead,
From total blazon to sunk yellow and retreating smoke-trails,
Between forkfuls of garden rubbish, the October sky's handbreadth
Telescoped and judged the world. And I suddenly saw
My meanings and ambitions run through on a cine-film, with the
handle
Turned too fast for a joke. Ichabod has an illuminated I,
Is a firework timed for a child's rapid wonder and immediate tiring.

Dry Sea

This would be a fine day if
And a blue pouring sea
And a rapture of swimming if
And a bask of sand-hot drying

If I ever any longer
Since those I love died or found alteration
Lived in the present tense
And not the conditional.

*

Who is there to tell?
When love fails, language fails.
I saw this day heavens opened
While all day long there fell
Blue radiance on the sea
But who is there to tell?
I saw it well
But none was there with me
Nor is there any left whom I could tell.
Heaven needs witnesses, whether God or friend,
Without such sharing, there is only
One blue day, and its end.

Hospital

Where dust-winds from the river blow
And the tall storeys block the dark
They took the body of my love
And caged her faltering lark.

Where crates of patient buildings rise
And stop just short of the green sky
They ticked her down the electric rows
One nameless light to lie.

Was time a steel and concrete frame
And pain a lift-shaft short of air?
Which way she went I cannot find,
There's no way down from there.

She, strangered from the starry trees
Into this terminus of cells
Came when the stars grew faint to please,
But finds what homeland else?

I try in vain the muttering doors
And cannot tell which way she left.
Far up above the evening sleeps
Insufferably soft.

In Memoriam
(for my mother)

My friend has died, I ran to you and said.
Console me - listen in your usual way,
Till, kindled by your sympathy, her gay
True self revives out of my memory's bed.

You who love life, and have so much to lend,
Talk of her, and your warmth will thaw her tomb.
But I had run into an empty room:
I could not speak, because you were that friend.

Sale of a House

Let it go under the hammer
Of the snow.
These winter roots no more my hazard.
Whether the smothered crocuses survive
Their over-hopefulness
Under the snake-limbed willow, hooped with closed peacock-trails,
It is not my hand will draw back this blanket:
Although its mood
Of putting hopes to bed
Seeps from a heaviside layer built long ago,
Payment of some cumulus debt this hour
Which I forgot and owe.

In the summer under the mulberry sun
Others will come by right
Where the fat leaves parcel the sky like a monk's margin
And the grass bleeds with abandoned fruit,
Ailanthus climbing heaven
Jack's beanstalk, plays thief go-between,
And the tapestry briar with its plush crucifix
Rosa Moyesii, rosa mundi
Of a pagan exquisiteness, smokes
Holy before the bonfire.
Whose sacrifice was not acceptable
Abel's or Cain's, we neither know.

Nor which I am, who drew
The sheet over their planter's face,
My gardener mother,
Displaced such diamond plans
In blue imagination's eyes
Which are bluest when the hope is least.
On that snow sheet words made no footmarks.
So let me go in peace
Father Christmas receding with a lantern
Having blessed the house,
Gentle duty which knows no other season.
I am under contract to be gone before the snow.

For A.Y.C.

Sleep well beyond the gentle sun,
Desk left, head bowed, hands laid aside,
The unfinished page left open wide
For others now to pause upon.
The last moment to fear
Was here, is gone.

So many things begun,
All hopes, all disappointments, find
This idleness their patient sum.
It must have seemed enough, at last,
To have no more to come
Except the past.

For My Parents

I can imagine you whom time divided
Set free by now to wander shores in hand:
For whom time's tyranny is ended,
You whose foreign fibres grew together
In a knot which the tree keeps, however outwards
And far apart from there the branches grew;
And the pull of the knot still there has drawn you
                                    back to it
First one, by this the other,
For even the dead feel hunger till the number
Of their elect can be completed.
No true election
Is nulled into rejection
By later mood's vicissitude.

What death has joined let no past part asunder.
And all in which one suffers solitude
By this be promised temporary:
The unshared impulse, ache of private wonder,
The cross-grained growths time would not marry -
At length you glimpsed the counterparts
Did tally,
In the great round of things, by which away
Becomes in the long run towards.
Run then to meet across your long gold sands.

Love Song for my people

In the spring louder than at other times,
The early spring with no leaves yet, though by
The sun there surely should be, by the length
Of days an end of cold seems promised,
Louder than at other times the voices sound
'Come back to us,
Why make do with so little happiness,
We at least loved you once; wherever
In time or out of time we are to be found
Come back, the rest is leafless ground.

What future summers promise more than declining
Rays? Freshness was long ago (which is
And ever shall be), do not confuse it
With temporary remission of the encroaching cloud,
With alleviation of the tarnish
Which began in earnest
When those for whom you made time green
Packed their desires and hopes
And between a night and a morning were no more seen.'

And call louder at some times of day and year than others
Not for readmittance, but against all shelter
As frail, except the final, where
Eyes of recognition shall have outlasted
The Proteus weather's last device.
In that still blue
Which next week early spring may suddenly guess at
But you I loved inhabit -
Where should I know you at home so rightfully
Now tides have done with you.

Call for me at last, over the water walking,
Out of the rain seeping on a mistbound night,
Talk to me at last in the tones of recognition
Without which all times and all spaces are alike
A void and expense of spirit, reach me at last
Your once warm hands, whether you are my past or future
You are the only meaning, the only lie
Is to say you never were; you know the place of meeting.

Though the house is dark and I the only one stirring
I shall not be afraid,
Nightgown-white down the passage or into the garden
By a moon-thin thread, the maze itself was the only
Great beast to be defeated
And the ways in are ways out, I shall not be lonely,
I have waited so long for you at the true beginning.

                              *

What if all time runs backwards from its source?
The best is first not last? Laboriously
Like a fish swimming upstream, one stems the flood.
How sheer a waterfall against us stood:
If you are my true loves, take breath with me
And leap to reach or die, beyond all laws.

Pembrokeshire Day

A huge cow browses the half-inch cliff
Dwarfing the sunny castle.
Hang-stomach heights
The harebells play with.
Time ticks, retracts, a genial sentry.

This bay was carved freehand
By certainties of casual force.
The child-gulls shriek and chatter
Have set up cricket stumps,
Will pack when the sun calls home.

Immense and tiny
Earth's crannies copy each others' features;
Worn by whatever deluge,
Her ancient smile spreads from the corners,
Waves that could kill turn ripples.

Sleek-limbed, a bronze-age blessed one
From high up here seen headlong
Streaks greedily for the siphoning edge
Over the bay's gold apron-stage,
Keels in.

Released for one.
Gull-moment of pure flight,
I wheel and choose that sea-drop ledge,
That iceberg-tipped striation,
Plunge purple-deep in that gulf stream -

Plummeting through time
Pearl-diving go
For riches of the green-womb past
Turned up suddenly incorruptible
(O pray for that, sad Brother

Saint Govan, halfway hermit,
Cliffhanger, by whose grace
I used a knee-worn bath this morning,
And the four-fist-clenched waves
Lifted me clear then back).

Now sandhill pines
Lose me in their identical private dells
A moon landscape
Colonised by hot papery bracken,
Lichen, round rabbit pellets;

My tent squats here,
Sleeps one, fends rain,
Swimsuit hangs from the pole,
Beside me singing in the wilderness
My kettle brews for consolation.

A courtier's palace hopes
I long ago resigned;
Now growing old
Think humans best cut down to size
And distanced by redeeming spaces.

Small enterprises
Like those of mice in corn
Pipe down now on the immense sand plains -
Dog and ball miniatures; the sundial bay
Wanes to a segment;

Yet goat-foot still in the long slow light
Among grey rocks and red
Picking Self-heal
Up to the topmost gate of sunset,
I turn as if tapped on the shoulder -

Nameless recognition
Stood for a hand's breadth
On the gate's blue side:
Streamed from one homing cloud,
Of many, one, full sail, making for All Souls' reef.

Trick of the light, who knows?
Wish of a ghost, two ghosts
Asunder once together under sky's wander-waste?
If ever real,
Then real for ever.

Turning home
I go slowly.
Watch in the low-tide lull
Two surfboard riders' long drawn out
Ink-marks, on the silver-lidded waves.

Draw on, sweet night.
The Queen's barge furls her cloaks
Round lords and beach-boys sandy eyed:
Whose time of madrigals was signalled
By stars my tent still peeps on.

Logudoro, Place of Gold
(A district of Sardinia)

Beyond the hills are hills,
Beyond the mountains are the mountains,
Home is past home
The sea is oversea.
Then how can there be endings
Beyond mending,
For us who colonise
Infinity?

No man is an Island

"For surely once, they feel, we were
Parts of a single continent." (Matthew Arnold)

There comes a time when the world stops unrolling
In widening whirls of green its lovely lands,
And no more infinite-lunged gusts come bowling
Down stripped for action sands,

A time when barns that gaped their doors for harvest
Creak shut on their great gains, or on their small
Husk heaps that hurt the hand, and even the farthest
Reach-hold of love must close, and count this all;

When what we are becomes a tide-left island
That shrinks into itself with every wave,
While the encroaching water white and silent
Claims back the lease it gave.

What wonder, then, I seek to cast my hawsers
Star-high, to track the sun's retreating flame,
To learn to walk the obliterating waters
Towards some twinkling coast without a name.

*   *   *

From Eliot's fifth quartet

In the dark at stairfall,
Under or aside from the weight of whispers
(Collecting one's coat after the party)
When the guest is greater than the dining
Yet declining might have been misconstrued,
These jejune considerations
(Locked suddenly in the stair cupboard)
Fuse, with a final
Dismembering of the evening's pattern,
Into a lifetime's loss
Acknowledged, while waiting
Among the humped coats and vacuum cleaners
(Wait, wait, wait, cried the spider)
For the returning maid to unlock the cupboard,
Dilatory, a long time coming -
If coming is the word for it.
Well, every lock-in is also a lock-out
In the last analysis,
Which is also the preamble,
So a dull time shall be had of it by all.
For time was is time will be,
And purl is plain from the other side,
And the true is the half true which is also the untrue,
And five past ten is ten past five
And six and fourpence is the same as four and sixpence
For the sufficiently pontifical mind
(Quickly, pocket the difference.
I have found my coat though not the exit).

*(This parody has been set to music by John Marsden, but it requires a
prepared piano.)*

My best Latin verse

Prodiga sis, feli sardam concede secundam

*(translates the saying "Give the cat another sardine and hang
the expense.")*

After Ascot

(written for a competition to describe the occasion
when 700 people leaving Ascot were breathalysed)

One should have come upon a horse
Of course.
No horse need give a fart
For the effronteries of the Force,
Its noble air-vents are too wide apart.

Look, there's Augusta, sweating gin,
Riding the clutch;
No sooner did this queue begin,
The Duke got out and she got in -
Doubt if that helps them much.

Whose is that Rolls?
Good grief! considering what
He's won today, the drinks he must have bought
Could jail a good few hundred souls.
He must have food for thought.

There's Reg
Trying a U-turn, with the Count.
Tame cars, that cannot leap a hedge,
Or even a soft verge -
My husband's peerage for a decent mount!

True horsepower never hangs the head.
You cannot breathalyse a
Thoroughbred.
Nor does it run amok because its rider
Has got champagne inside her.

By Jove! that's lucky:
The gate to Nigel's field is open.
Among friends' cars bogged down and mucky
He and his gorgeous Porsch' sit mopin'.
"A HORSCH IS BETTER, DUCKY"

Reading and Partly Reading
(An evening with the small ads)

Boy's 24 wheel bicycle
Deep chest freezer standing in garden, needs muffler
Gate-legged three-piece in dark navy for tall man,
     fourth leg missing,
Electric chair for that surprise relative's visit
Home freezing, and other books on the British way of life
Free, 50 yards continuous bodybelting to successful
     dismantler of present wearer
Back-seat driver needs front-loading partner to pass Test
Hearth-side chair by Critique, in cutting moquette
High-speed, self-charging Don't Do It Yourself kit
Have It Yourself kittens (adoptable)
Always wanted, unisex donors of spare parts
Collapsible pink baby, complete with bathwater
     (genuine reason for disposal),
Pram with drop-side toys, non-recoverable
Screaming kettle for use as Mothercare safety valve
Nearly new padded headboard, with cell.

Mallard Immaculate
(seen in the Cambridge Backs)

She had nine ducklings,
All well grown, in formation on the steeply sloping bank,
Mostly in pairs, playfully dishevelling each others'
Heads, but keeping in order,
Land drill echoes water drill -
Except that they were in front:
She had drawn herself up behind them
Tall as she'd go,
On parade, webbing immaculate, webs carefully in First ballet
position,
Beak held musket-straight.
Only her eyes sometimes rolled inwards
With the sheer triumph of it all,
Allowing her an introvert moment.
She knew perfectly well about the passers by
Stopping to admire
More openly than she could lose rank by doing.
Either there is no such thing as consciousness
Or -
"She's proud", I said to my neighbour at the railing.
He smiled, being a person of perception,
And said "No question."

"The thing about the spring"

The thing about the spring
Is that things are supposed to be getting better all the time.
These rolls upon rolls of cotton wool
So grey you could almost call them blue, if you didn't remember
      what blue was,
Are supposed to be the packaging round the sun's birthday present
      to us all.
These lumps of sodden clay straddled with dead grass
Are supposed to burst into a mosaic of intricate leaves and petals
Overnight, like a London park when the instant prefab job has
      been done on it.
As for the other things that get called Spring,
Youth (forsooth, in an unemployment era)
Being in love, wanting to write a poem -
Interminable wrappings of disappointment merely,
With no present or presence inside,
Like Peer Gynt's onion?
Yet if that were so
Even onions would not bother to wrap up against this cold
As if knowing themselves precious.

Waking

This dazzling sun
Surely life-giver
Floods room, floods earth
Prodigally long -
-forgotten how;
Then why
No answering spring
Of self, of buds?
I know
Before I look,
That white light is snow.

*

Extra Time

Precious, this spring, by the extra measure
Of its hard birth from ice.
Could still revert inside the womb-cold,
An easier route than upwards
Strenuously wooing the withdrawn sun
Hymened with silver.
Mornings should not be misgivings.
Warmth steals lazily, sleepy fingers
Risked outside the blanket.
Oh when when when fling off this covering?
My soul was always, yet never wished to be
A late riser.

So bridegroom sun has come to say goodbye
And I still fast.
Time Will Be and Time Is have all but passed
me by.

I laboured up the hill of heavenly truth:
In Greece, wrote feminism with a slipped disc;
Squandered my prettiest time in war, whose risk
One knew was death of youth.

This August cannot last: seeks to atone
For a haggard May.
Intimations of joyfulness fill the day
Saying none should sit alone.

I did not want the central place, the bride's;
I wanted friends and feasting and glad lights.
But though I have trimmed my lantern with steadfastness
I am stumbling in an indoor darkness.

If in the house I sit,
At Home seems Nowhere, so where's anywhere?
Remembered people through my mirrors flit
But I am missing there.

The garden has its birds its fish its song
At least no mirrors: but a greater need
Of celebration, earth and air to greet
Me with "here you belong":
Not with the frost's anon.

August End

This sweet and finished time
Should suit old friends conversing;
Sun's gold dispersing
Its handshake to freed birds,
The scent of phlox rehearsing
Wiseacre aftertastes
Like distant rhyme.

So much is safe (or are
Frosts retrospective?
Then justice should restore
Some treasures jettisoned);
Patience is a perspective,
The price of it
The sadness of things distance-ended.

I seem to touch last year
With deckchair-lazy fingers;
Elusive like pond fish
Dead friends malinger.
This time of year should suit
Eternity's conversing,
But the veil of ah, no substance, has no mercy.

Evening Primrose

A primrose evening, soft as gold:
Whose closing petals counsel peace,
Say after long delayed release
I should be glad to fold.

A placid sea, whose ancient face
Accepting night looks grey as dawn
While sense of time and place
Is quietly withdrawn.

How a day's death becomes it more
As the year gentles towards its close:
I am long past being one of those
For whom untimely death could be in store.

Yet, still containing every age,
I cannot help remembering
How strong the light was on the page
Of spring.

*

I shall elude you, jaws.
I have a place to go
That is young and lovely
Though the stars fall,
Though man unkind consume his whole
Inheritance, in a mass anguish.
This place I have has been,
And even God cannot unmake past time,
So Milton promises;
Back shall I run
Where the sea breaks clean on the unpolluted sand,
And promises I made there
Have, despite all, yes, though I hear
Mockeries of cave laughter, have in some curious
Perverse way, been kept.
(Granted the basic failures
Each of us knows of, by the end.)

Water-Drip

Each steepled chime
Heart takes a hammering.
Don't ask mortality to last:
Death's a great blessing.

Stubble Burning

The rest is Autumn.
And tired of summer, the year is glad
Of earlier darkness, of mist dimming
The sun's ardency, of almost windlessness
In a warm, fruitful exhaustion.

The sun's borrowers now pay back
Their golden debts, richer than sun now
In inglowing colours:
September roses
Late cousins, leaving take their time,
Keep ashen petals long intact.

Black flakes from stubble burning
Snow down, black swansdown.
Oh all my daydreams
Incinerate as briskly!
Broadcast your brittleness
Carbon hydrogen oxygen
Some chance real gronth
Might recombine your crude elements
Outside my time cycle,
You unharvestable residue of a life.
There is a law of conservation
So why should anyone lament endings.

I am a Celt

One can recognise the symptoms of an ending:
Déjà vu quality,
Longterm echoes are caught up with,
Ah that subdominant chord
Organising the distances which in middle life were out of view.
A person from long ago came to stay with me
And was unchanged,
And I am unchanged,
Which is why there could be little point in elaborating
        on me further -
After recapitulation, a graceful exit.
Possibly something was learnt from all that stressful
And fragmented section they dignify as development -
Possibly not.
I like tunes
Whether from Dylan's chimneys
Or the bagpipes in my ancient blood.
Tunes are what has staying power;
After the scurryings to and fro,
The confabulations, the risks of sabotage, in a word
        as I have said the development section,
The inventor of the tune always knew why he liked it,
Even if others seemed to require a fuller unfolding.
I am coming over the hill on this fine early summer morning
Singing my own tune
Like the shepherds and the milkmaids in their far-off habits
Who bore these genes before me;
Like the butterfly, mole and sparrow
Scornful of interruption
By a crass car-wheel.
Heaven holds completed phrases
Whatever the –

Astronomy

Most of its course my Plough has run,
Yet August still has shooting stars -
Amazing lucid intervals

The Sword the Swan the Lyre the Sled
Signs that I steered by long ago
Still directly overhead

In steady state exploding still,
Making the dark light's pacemaker.
O could I trust all bright things so

By contraries refreshed outride
Their safe-conducting negative,
And light-years passed arrive, arrive.

INDEX

page

Clare, aged about 30, drawn by her brother Adrian Campbell

New Page

A NIKKI PAGE MYSTERY
BOOK 1

SHERYL STEINES